Dan Gutman

My Favorite Writer

Gillian Richardson

WEIGL PUBLISHERS INC.

Published by Weigl Publishers Inc.
350 5th Avenue, Suite 3304, PMB 6G
New York, NY 10118-0069
USA
Web site: www.weigl.com

Library of Congress Cataloging-in-Publication Data

Richardson, Gillian.
  Dan Gutman / by Gillian Richardson.
     p. cm. -- (My favorite writer)
  Includes index.
  ISBN 1-59036-284-5 (hard cover : alk. paper) -- ISBN 1-59036-290-X
(soft cover : alk. paper)
  1. Gutman, Dan--Juvenile literature. 2. Authors, American--20th
century--Juvenile literature. 3. Creative writing--Juvenile literature. I.
Title. II. Series.
  PS3557.U8855Z85 2005
  813'.54--dc22

                                              2004029926

Project Coordinator
Tina Schwartzenberger

Substantive Editor
Frances Purslow

Design
Terry Paulhus

Layout
Jeff Brown
Kathryn Livingstone

Photo Researcher
Kim Winiski

Printed in the United States of America
1 2 3 4 5 6 7 8 9 0 09 08 07 06 05

Contents

Dan Gutman

MILESTONES

1955 Born on October 19 in New York City

1977 Graduates from Rutgers University with a degree in psychology

1980 Moves to New York City

1982 Starts a magazine called *Video Games Player*

1983 Marries Nina Wallace

1985 Becomes a **freelance writer** and publishes his first book, *The Greatest Games*

1990 Nina gives birth to a son, Sam

1993 Begins writing books for children

1994 First children's novel, *They Came From Centerfield*, is published

1995 Daughter Emma is born

2000 Publishes *Landslide! A Kid's Guide to the U.S. Elections*

2004 Fourth and final book in the million-dollar series, *The Million Dollar Strike*, is published

No one becomes a writer of children's books overnight. Just ask Dan Gutman. Dan always wanted to be a writer, but it took 15 years before he discovered the fun and excitement of writing for children. Dan's many fans enjoy his stories about sports, history, and an added twist of **fantasy**. His characters are ordinary children given imaginative challenges that lead to funny situations. Would you like to travel back in time to meet a famous person? Qwerty Stevens travels through time in Dan Gutman's time-travel adventure books. With more than forty children's books to his credit, Dan has grown and changed as a writer. He is constantly inspired by children's imaginations. Dan's readers admire his never-give-up attitude. Anything can happen in Dan's books when fact, **fiction**, and a generous amount of imagination and humor are mixed together.

Early Childhood

> "I discovered it wasn't that I disliked reading, it was that I just disliked reading things that didn't interest me."
> **Dan Gutman**

Dan Gutman was born in New York City on October 19, 1955. When Dan was 1 year old, his family moved to Newark, New Jersey. His father, Sid, worked in advertising. His mother, Adeline, stayed home to look after Dan and his sister, Lucy.

Dan's favorite childhood hobbies included playing with friends and watching television. He especially enjoyed comedy shows such as *Get Smart*, and movies starring Woody Allen or the Pink Panther. Dan's interest in writing funny stories probably began to develop during these years.

Dan enjoyed school. His love of learning new things influenced his time-travel books. The books include facts about the time in history when the story takes place and the famous people his fictional hero, Qwerty Stevens, meets in his adventures.

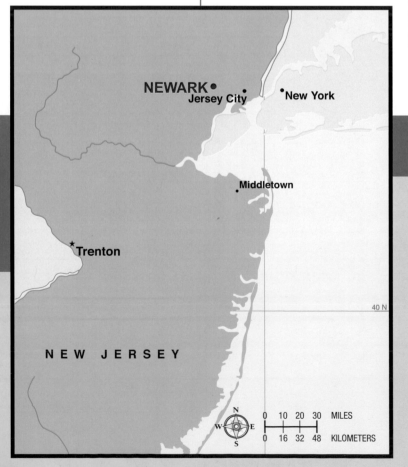

Newark is the largest city in New Jersey.

Strangely, Dan found reading boring and difficult when he began school. His mother even bought comic books to tempt him to read. The comic books met with little success. Still, Dan received good grades in English class.

Other students often teased Dan because he was the shortest and skinniest child in class. This bothered Dan until he was an adult. Although he was not a good athlete, Dan liked sports. By fourth grade, Dan's growing interest in baseball changed his attitude toward reading. He was a loyal New York Mets fan. Dan began spending time at the public library near his home, researching the statistics for Babe Ruth and other legendary baseball players. Dan's passion to learn more about baseball history led to reading about this topic. Soon, he turned to books to learn about other new things.

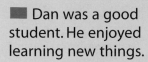

■ Dan and his sister, Lucy, played together in the Mount Vernon Park.

■ Dan was a good student. He enjoyed learning new things.

Growing Up

When Dan was 10 or 11 years old, his parents bought him a darkroom kit for his birthday. The kit contained all the necessary chemicals and equipment to develop photographs. Dan created a darkroom in his basement room. Dan remembers that he enjoyed experimenting with different ways of developing his photographs to create special effects. He sometimes scratched negatives to see how the photographs would develop. For a short time, Dan even wanted to be a photographer when he grew up. Dan still enjoys photography. He takes many photos of his family, especially when they are on vacation.

Dan enjoyed experimenting with different ways of developing photographs to create special effects.

When Dan was 12 years old, his father unexpectedly left the family. Dan returned home from a Little-League game one day to find his mom and sister alone. He did not see his father for 10 years.

Coping with his parents' divorce greatly affected Dan. He frequently removes the father from the stories he writes. Sometimes the father suddenly appears at the end of a story. Dan's characters show strength and **resilience** in single-parent families. Through his writing, Dan shows that such changes are not the end of the world.

Dan did not appreciate it at the time, but now he admires his mother's strength. She had been a homemaker, but suddenly faced the task of raising her son and daughter alone. She took secretarial courses and learned to drive. She used these new skills to raise her children.

Inspired to Write

Dan learned that he could overcome serious obstacles such as his parents' divorce when he was a teenager. He presents difficult challenges for his story characters, mixing in light-hearted fantasy elements to give his books humor. Like Dan, his characters do not give up. They find solutions to their problems.

Dan and Lucy spent time with their mother and grandparents while growing up.

Dan's high-school years were busy. He was involved in many activities and socialized with a group of friends. Dan continued to play sports. For a few years, he played tennis.

Dan's writing skills emerged while he worked on the school newspaper as a writer and photographer. He loved the thrill of shooting action photos from the sidelines at football games. He held the position of yearbook photography **editor** in his senior year. Dan's interest in photography led to a summer job. For two summers, he taught photography at a camp for physically challenged children.

Dan remained a good student, although he continued to struggle with math in high school and in college. Algebra, geometry, trigonometry, and calculus—forms of math that use a combination of numbers and letters—confused him.

"I didn't start writing until I was about 25 . . . . But I always found that writing came naturally to me."
Dan Gutman

Dan worked at Camp Oakhurst in Oakhurst, New Jersey, for four summers. He was the photo specialist in 1977 and 1978.

Sports continued to interest Dan while he grew up. Professional sports offered action and team spirit. Dan has always enjoyed sports because "it's the only kind of entertainment where nobody knows the outcome in advance.... In sports, anything can happen. I'm attracted to the drama of that."

While Dan writes about several sports, he writes about baseball more than any other sport. Baseball is Dan's favorite sport. He feels that it is more **strategic** than other sports. Dan also says that baseball is easy to write about because "there's plenty of time when the players are standing around trying to figure out what to do next."

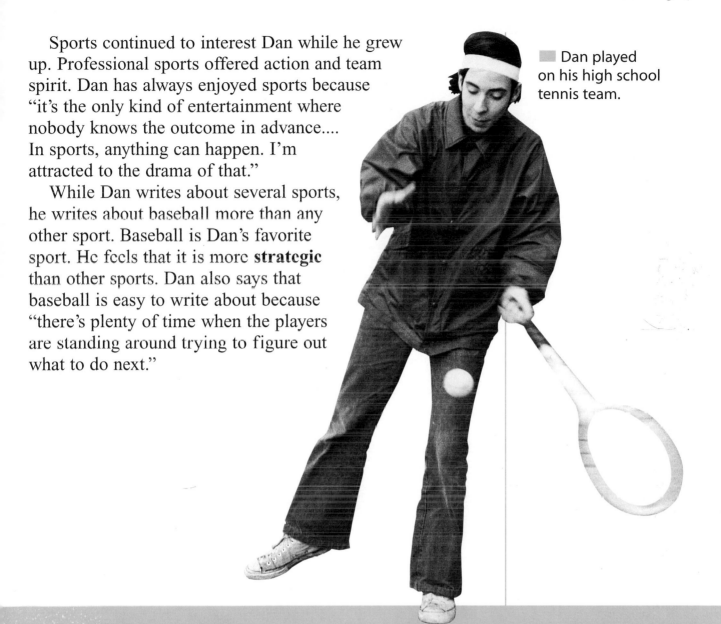

Dan played on his high school tennis team.

Favorite Authors

When Dan began reading for pleasure, he enjoyed the stories of British author, Roald Dahl. Roald Dahl wrote the fantasy stories *Charlie and the Chocolate Factory* and *James and the Giant Peach*. Dan likes to include fantastic **plots** in his own writing. Gary Paulsen, an American writer, is another of Dan's favorite authors. Gary Paulsen's dramatic survival adventures, such as *Hatchet*, *Dogsong*, and *Brian's Winter*, test the courage of the heroes. Dan's main characters use their personal strengths to resolve **conflicts** as well. To satisfy his love of humor, Dan enjoys Gordon Korman and Carl Hiassen novels.

Learning the Craft

Dan enjoyed the creativity of writing letters.

Dan went to college, but he was uncertain about his future career. He earned a psychology degree from Rutgers University in New Brunswick, New Jersey, in 1977. Then, he attended **graduate school**. Before long, Dan realized that he did not enjoy psychology. He really wanted to write.

Dan enjoyed the creativity of writing letters. He wondered what kind of writing could become a full-time job. Dan began writing humorous essays in 1978. Two years later, he moved to New York City, the gathering place for many hopeful writers. Dan admired humorous writers such as Art Buchwald and Erma Bombeck. He wanted to follow in their footsteps and be a successful humor writer.

Dan sent his essays to magazines and newspapers. His magazine articles met with limited success. Dan tried writing **screenplays**. He sent book ideas to publishers. Dan even submitted his photographs to children's magazines. His photographs were published in the magazines *Cracked* and *Crazy*. Still, Dan received far more rejections than acceptances.

Dan attended Rutgers University in New Jersey. The school was founded as Queens College in 1766 and was renamed Rutgers College in 1825. The college became a university in 1945.

It was difficult to pay the bills on the unpredictable earnings of an unknown freelance writer. Unknown freelance writers do not earn much money. They sometimes have difficulty finding work. Fortunately, Dan had **persistence** and determination. He also had a sense of humor. Dan refused to give up on his dream. He believed strongly in his writing abilities.

Dan had a goal—to have a book published by the time he was 30 years old. He wrote constantly. Dan believed his writing was just as good as what he read in newspapers, magazines, and books. After hundreds of rejection letters, Dan was very frustrated. He wondered which direction he should take with his writing to achieve success.

Inspired to Write

Dan believes that his books are unique because he never formally learned the rules of writing. He preferred to follow the path of great writers. Dan believes these authors did not follow **formulas**, but broke new ground with their work.

Although Dan enjoyed photography, he felt he was not very good at it. That is one of the reasons he became a writer.

Getting Published

In 1982, video games became popular. Dan created a successful magazine called *Video Games Player*. After a couple of years, the magazine was renamed *Computer Games*. During his years as a magazine editor—the only "real" job that Dan says he had—he wrote articles about computers. He even had a **syndicated** column in the *Philadelphia Inquirer* and the *Miami Herald* newspapers. Being known as a computer expert did not feel right to Dan. His heart was not in computers.

While working on *Computer Games*, Dan hired an **illustrator** named Nina Wallace to draw for the magazine. Dan met Nina at Times Square. He took her to a video arcade to show her what he wanted her to draw. They got along very well. Nina and Dan married in 1983.

The computer magazine ceased publication in 1985. Dan used his experience to write about other topics for magazines such as *Newsweek*, *Science Digest*, and *USA Today*.

The Publishing Process

Publishing companies receive hundreds of **manuscripts** from authors each year. Only a few manuscripts become books. Publishers must be sure that a manuscript will sell many copies. As a result, publishers reject most of the manuscripts they receive.

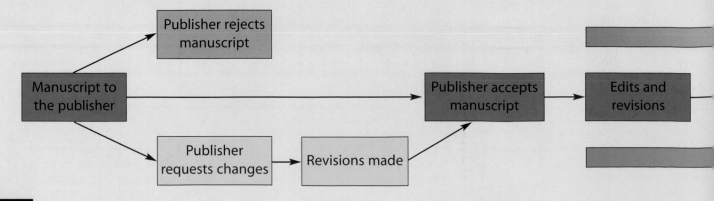

When Dan began to write about sports, he achieved his goal. His first book, *The Greatest Games*, was published in 1985 when Dan was 30 years old.

In 1990, an important event in Dan's life changed the direction of his writing. Sam, his son, was born. Dan read children's books to Sam and discovered that the books were fun to read. Dan thought children's books were probably fun to write as well. He decided to try writing books for children.

At first, Dan wrote **nonfiction** books about sports. Dan's first children's novel, *They Came from Centerfield*, was published in 1994. Once Dan began visiting schools, he saw the excitement his books brought to children. Dan realized that this was what he had been working toward his whole life. Writing for children was fun and challenged his creative abilities. He gained inspiration from his young audiences who showed their appreciation with enthusiastic laughter and fan mail.

Inspired to Write

Dan believed that his novel, *Honus & Me*, was special, even though it was rejected ten times. Dan received feedback from children during school visits. He believed that he knew what children liked to read. He persisted and finally found a publisher who agreed with him. *Honus & Me* is now a bestseller and award winner.

Once a manuscript has been accepted, it goes through many stages before it is published. Often, authors change their work to follow an editor's suggestions. Once the book is published, some authors receive royalties. This is money based on book sales.

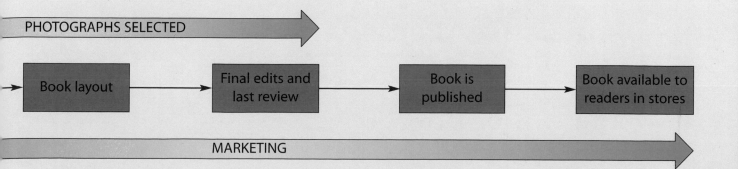

PHOTOGRAPHS SELECTED →

Book layout → Final edits and last review → Book is published → Book available to readers in stores

MARKETING →

Writer Today

Dan Gutman is an active, full-time writer. He no longer writes for adults. Dan prefers the fun and excitement of creating imaginative stories for children. His work keeps him busy. Dan loves traveling across the country to visit up to 100 schools each year for presentations and workshops.

Dan's home is in Haddonfield, New Jersey. His wife, Nina, works at home, too. She is a graphic designer. His son, Sam, loves skateboarding. Sam does not enjoy traditional sports such as baseball. Dan's daughter, Emma, was born in 1995. She often helps her father by reading and commenting on his manuscripts. The family shares its home with Scrumpy, the cat.

Dan enjoys the freedom of being his own boss. His days usually include a morning writing session that begins at nine o'clock. Sometimes he writes on his laptop computer while sitting in the backyard.

■ When Dan is not working, he spends most of his time with his family.

After a noon break, Dan may make telephone calls, answer e-mail, or visit the library to research his next book. Many of Dan's stories include factual details that must be accurate. Readers can learn about the U.S. government, for example, by reading *The Kid Who Ran for President*.

Dan enjoys spending time with his family. His hobbies include riding his bicycle and playing guitar. He also enjoys watching movies and traveling. These activities distract Dan while he waits to hear if his books have been accepted by publishers or readers. Months may pass before the book is released. It takes even longer for **reviews** to be released. Then there is even more waiting for the sales results.

Dan's newest book in the Baseball Card Adventure series, *Abner & Me*, was released in early 2005. *The Million Dollar Strike* will delight bowling fans. He has also created a series for younger readers called My Weird School. The first title in this series is *Miss Daisy is Crazy*. Dan plans to write at least twelve books in the series.

Dan has no plans to retire. He enjoys writing humor, fantasy, and sports books for children.

Dan's daughter, Emma, inspired the My Weird School series.

Popular Books

D an spends a great deal of time writing for children ages 7 to 12. Most of his books are published in series. He continues to write new stories for each series.

Qwerty Stevens, Back in Time: The Edison Mystery

Dan Gutman uses time travel to teach history to young readers. In this series, 13-year-old Qwerty Stevens comes across devices that transport him back in time where he witnesses important events in history.

In *The Edison Mystery*, he finds a strange box buried in his backyard. When Qwerty connects the box to his computer, he travels back in time. He arrives in Thomas Edison's laboratory in 1879, just as the inventor is trying to develop the electric light bulb.

Thomas Edison's laboratory in New Jersey is a national historic site. It is near Dan's childhood home in Newark, and he visited it often. Dan decided to link the past and the present in this mystery/historical adventure. While readers puzzle over how Qwerty will get back to his home in present time, they will also learn about Thomas Edison's inventions.

Miss Daisy Is Crazy

In this book from the My Weird School series, A. J. is not keen on school, especially math and reading. He is amazed when his new grade 2 teacher, Miss Daisy, claims to hate the same things. A. J. and his classmates decide that Miss Daisy is cool, and that they should keep the fact that she cannot spell, read, add, or multiply from Principal Klutz. They vow to help her, by explaining what they know about reading and arithmetic.

When the class has the idea of buying the school so that they can make their own rules, Miss Daisy gets the principal to agree to their idea—sort of. If all the students read one million pages, the principal will turn the school into an arcade for one night. Will kids who do not like reading take up the challenge?

The Million Dollar Shot

Dan often starts a book with a "big idea." In *The Million Dollar Shot*, Eddie "Air" Ball tries to win a chance to sink a million-dollar free throw at halftime in the National Basketball Association finals. To win the chance, Eddie must win a poetry contest. The problem is that Eddie is not very good at writing poetry. However, his best friend is. With Annie "Oakley" Stokely's help, the money may be within reach.

They Came from Centerfield

Dan's first book of humorous fiction for children is *They Came from Centerfield*. In this imaginative science-fiction tale, Bloop Jones and his baseball team, the Silent But Deadly (SBD), meet their match when a group of aliens arrive to challenge their winning record.

Johnny Hangtime

Johnny Hangtime is one of Dan's favorite books. The main character is 13-year-old Johnny. He is the son of a legendary Hollywood stuntman. After his father's death during a dangerous stunt, Johnny feels drawn to the same career. He acts in fight scenes, jumps off buildings, and falls from airplanes for teen movie idol, Ricky Corvette. Johnny's part in the movies must be kept secret to protect Ricky's image. The day comes when Johnny must face the same stunt that killed his father: going over Niagara Falls. Can he do it? As he prepares for his toughest challenge, a surprise awaits Johnny. If you want to know the secrets behind movie stunts, you will enjoy this novel.

AWARDS
The Million Dollar Shot

1999–2000 Sequoia Book Award (Oklahoma)

1999–2000 Nutmeg Children's Book Award (Connecticut)

1999–2000 Volunteer State Book Award (Tennessee)

2000–2001 Iowa Children's Choice Award

2000–2001 Maud Hart Lovelace Award (Minnesota)

2002–2003 California Young Reader Medal

Honus & Me

As a young boy, Dan dreamed of playing left field for the New York Mets. Although he never achieved this goal, Dan's love of baseball influences many of his stories. In this first Baseball Card Adventure book, baseball fan Joe Stoshack finds the world's most valuable baseball card—a 1909 Honus Wagner—when he is cleaning out an attic. The card is Joe's key to the past, where he meets up with the baseball hero and lives his dreams.

The Kid Who Ran for President

In this story, 12-year-old Judson Moon runs for U.S. president. His former babysitter is his running mate, and his best friend is his campaign manager. The story idea came to Dan when he learned that Bob Dole was a presidential candidate at age 72. Dan wondered if someone very young could run for president. The sequel to this book, *The Kid Who Became President*, tells of Judson's first year in office. Judson's largest challenge comes when he must face a mad South American **dictator**. A nonfiction book also grew from the research for this series. Dan wrote *Landslide! A Kid's Guide to the U.S. Election* because of the interest generated by these two novels.

AWARDS
Honus & Me
2000–2001 California Young Reader Medal

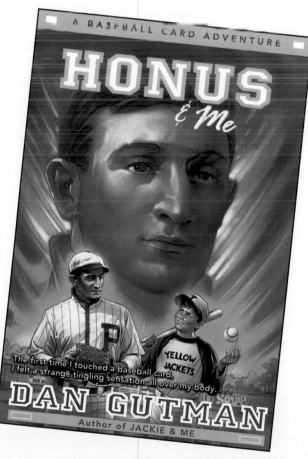

Creative Writing Tips

There are no right or wrong story ideas. Writing can be hard work, but it is exciting to create something original. Here are some tips to think about as you write.

Stay Alert for Ideas

Ideas for stories and nonfiction writing are everywhere. Dan Gutman finds ideas by reading, observing, and listening. He reads newspapers and listens to the radio. He also watches television programs, especially the ones he knows children enjoy best. Dan is a movie fan, too. Even Dan's children offer suggestions for his books. A video game scene in *The Kid Who Became President* was the brain wave of his son, Sam. Dan finds his school visits a great source of new ideas, too.

Stretch That Idea

With a little imagination, you can create a plot from a simple idea. Place an ordinary character in an extraordinary situation. Plan lots of trouble for your character. Add more characters, then dream of ways for your characters to solve their problems.

Dan writes his books in an office in his home.

Organize

Whether you are writing a story or a report for school, whether you like to use paper and pen or work on a computer, organization is important. Dan Gutman uses index cards to keep track of the information he collects while researching. He takes careful **jot notes** as he gathers facts. Later, Dan sorts them by topics. He might combine similar topics that will appear in the same chapter of a book. Dan has found that this method works for writing fiction and nonfiction.

Research

It takes time to write a good story or book. It takes Dan up to 4 months to write a nonfiction book, including research time. Fiction may take less time—2 or 3 months. Dan likes to include facts in his fiction, which often requires more research.

Make It Your Best: Revise

Dan spends a great deal of time planning and thinking before he actually begins writing. Then, Dan writes a first **draft**. The story is not finished at this stage. The most difficult part of writing can be rewriting. Every manuscript needs revisions to improve the text. Dan works closely with his editor when rewriting. He finds rewriting can be more difficult than creating the original draft. Dan suggests writers keep working until their story is the best it can be.

Inspired to Write

Networking with other writers keeps Dan Gutman aware of events and changes in his chosen field of work. He belongs to the Society of Children's Book Writers and Illustrators. Children's writers are like a big family. Each member is ready and willing to offer support and encouragement to others.

Writing a Biography Review

A biography is an account of an individual's life that is written by another person. Some people's lives are very interesting. In school, you may be asked to write a biography review. The first thing to do when writing a biography review is to decide whom you would like to learn about. Your school library or community library will have a large selection of biographies from which to choose.

Are you interested in an author, a sports figure, an inventor, a movie star, or a president? Finding the right book is your first task. Whether you choose to write your review on a biography of Dan Gutman or another person, the task will be similar.

Begin your review by writing the title of the book, the author, and the person featured in the book. Then, start writing about the main events in the person's life. Include such things as where the person grew up and what his or her childhood was like. You will want to add details about the person's adult life, such as whether he or she married or had children. Next, write about what you think makes this person special. What kinds of experiences influenced this individual? For instance, did he or she grow up in unusual circumstances? Was the person determined to accomplish a goal? Include any details that surprised you.

A concept web is a useful research tool. Use the concept web on the right to begin researching your biography review.

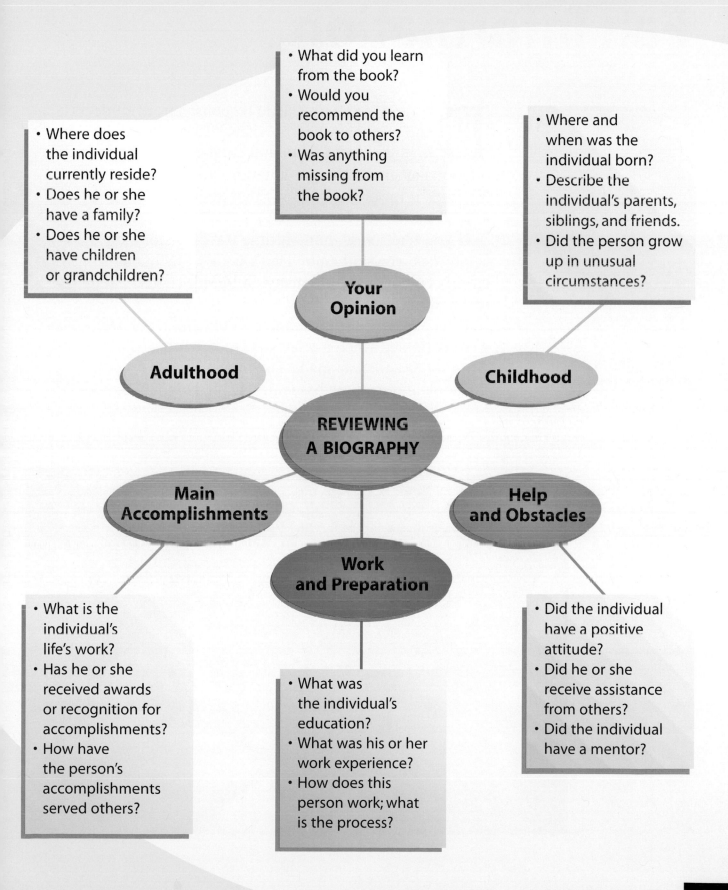

- Where does the individual currently reside?
- Does he or she have a family?
- Does he or she have children or grandchildren?

- What did you learn from the book?
- Would you recommend the book to others?
- Was anything missing from the book?

- Where and when was the individual born?
- Describe the individual's parents, siblings, and friends.
- Did the person grow up in unusual circumstances?

Your Opinion

Adulthood

Childhood

REVIEWING A BIOGRAPHY

Main Accomplishments

Help and Obstacles

Work and Preparation

- What is the individual's life's work?
- Has he or she received awards or recognition for accomplishments?
- How have the person's accomplishments served others?

- What was the individual's education?
- What was his or her work experience?
- How does this person work; what is the process?

- Did the individual have a positive attitude?
- Did he or she receive assistance from others?
- Did the individual have a mentor?

25

Fan Information

Dan receives enthusiastic responses from students and teachers when he visits schools. He is in high demand for personal appearances. Dan often makes up to 100 presentations each school year. He finds it rewarding to know that he inspires his fans to read more.

If you like sports, humor, time travel, history, or celebrities, you will enjoy Dan's books. His books have been honored with many children's choice awards and nominations.

Fans of Dan's award-winning book, *Honus & Me*, were delighted when a television movie titled *The Winning Season* was made. The movie is based on the book and features baseball legend, Honus Wagner.

Dan spends about 80 days each year visiting schools. He enjoys meeting his fans.

Dan has published more than forty children's books. Many children consider Dan Gutman a **role model** as they tackle life's challenges. His own heroes include "creative people who grew and changed over time." These heroes include the Beatles, Thomas Edison, and Stephen Spielberg. Dan admires firefighters, teachers, librarians, and others who work to help others. Dan's best advice is "never give up."

Dan Gutman
Children's Book Author

Hi! My name is Dan Gutman and I'm the author of many children's books, mostly about sports. I'm so glad you chose to visit my site. If you're a teacher, librarian, media specialist, or PTA member, you'll find a lot of information about my books and my school visits here. There are also articles about how to plan an author visit, and suggestions on how you can use sports to teach other subjects in your school. If you're a student and you want to do a book report about one of my books, you'll find plenty of stuff here to help you. Information about me and my books. Book excerpts. A chapter of a book I'm

WEB LINKS

Dan Gutman's Home Page

www.dangutman.com

Dan's Web site is packed with information about his writing life, his books, and advice to young people who aspire to be writers.

Quiz

Q: When and where was Dan Gutman born?

1

A: October 19, 1955, in New York City.

2

Q: What was Dan's favorite sport when he was a child?

A: Baseball

WHERE'D YOU GET THAT BEARD?

3

Q: Which of Dan's hobbies began with a birthday gift from his parents?

A: Dan received a darkroom kit and began to develop photographs.

4

Q: Does Dan use his photography skills today?

A: Yes, he takes photographs of his family.

5

Q: What was Dan's first goal as a writer? Did he reach it?

A: He wanted to publish a book by age 30. Yes, he published *The Greatest Games* in 1985, when he was 30 years old.

6

Q: What are the names of Dan's two children?

A: Sam and Emma

7

Q: Why did Dan begin writing for children?

A: He enjoyed reading to his son, Sam.

8

Q: Where does Dan write?

A: He writes at home in Haddonfield, New Jersey.

9

Q: Who inspired Dan's young reader series, My Weird School?

A: His daughter, Emma

10

Q: How many books has Dan Gutman written for children?

A: More than 40

Writing Terms

This glossary will introduce you to some of the main terms in the field of writing. Understanding these common writing terms will allow you to discuss your ideas about books and writing with others.

action: the moving events of a work of fiction

antagonist: the person in the story who opposes the main character

autobiography: a history of a person's life written by that person

biography: a written account of another person's life

character: a person in a story, poem, or play

climax: the most exciting moment or turning point in a story

episode: a short piece of action, or scene, in a story

fiction: stories about characters and events that are not real

foreshadow: hinting at something that is going to happen later in the book

imagery: a written description of a thing or idea that brings an image to mind

narrator: the speaker of the story who relates the events

nonfiction: writing that deals with real people and events

novel: published writing of considerable length that portrays characters within a story

plot: the order of events in a work of fiction

protagonist: the leading character of a story; often a likable character

resolution: the end of the story, when the conflict is settled

scene: a single episode in a story

setting: the place and time in which a work of fiction occurs

theme: an idea that runs throughout a work of fiction

Glossary

conflicts: problems that fictional characters face

dictator: a person who rules a country without sharing power or consulting others

draft: a rough copy of something written

editor: a person who makes changes in a book

fantasy: a story with characters, places, or events that are very unusual and unrealistic

fiction: stories about characters and events that are not real

formulas: sets of rules, or patterns, to follow

freelance writer: a writer who works on his or her own, not for an employer

graduate school: a school that grants master's degrees and/or doctorates, degrees that are more advanced than a bachelor's degree

illustrator: an artist who creates pictures for books, magazines, or other publications

jot notes: brief notes of facts found in research

manuscripts: drafts of stories before they are published

networking: socializing with people in the same career

nonfiction: writing that deals with real people and events

persistence: not giving up

plots: the order of events in works of fiction

resilience: ability to recover quickly from illness or depression

reviews: opinions

role model: a person who serves as an inspiration to others

screenplays: outline or script of a movie

strategic: requires planning

syndicated: sold to several publications at once

Index

Photo Credits

Cover: courtesy of Dan Gutman
Corbis/Lee Snider/Photo Images: page 12; courtesy of Dan Gutman: pages 1, 3, 4, 7L, 7R, 8L, 8R, 9, 10, 11, 13, 16, 17, 21, 22, 26, 28; courtesy of HarperCollins Publishers: page 19; courtesy of Hyperion Books: page 20; courtesy of Simon and Schuster: page 18.